AF417487

Praise for *The Willow Weepings*

"*The Willow Weepings* is a poetry collection like no other. It is a piece of art itself that enlightens you with a love for nature that may have be lying dormant inside of you or further connect you to the synched breaths with the trees, and allows you to explore love and heartbreak in a new light, as a warm bulb illuminating a room that feels both confining and ever-expanding. This book is an adventure we dive into about what makes us, us: our emotions and the nature we come from." — Flor Ana, Author of *A Moth Fell In Love With The Moon*

"*The Willow Weepings* perfectly bridges nature and poetry. Kendall Hope has created a masterpiece through her imagery, vulnerability, and expression of the natural world. I was continuously astonished and surprised throughout, wanting more after finishing the book. One of the most beautiful books of poetry I have ever read, Hope's work is tempestuous and unforgettable. — Amelie Honeysuckle, Author of *What Once Was An Inside Out Rainbow*

"*The Willow Weepings* feels like walking through a forest with a dear friend as she tells me the stories of her life. Of those she's loved, of those she's lost, of the flowers she admires and the reasons why. Hope has a singular way of taking something as seemingly ordinary as sea grass, or a luna moth, or snowdrops and forget-me-nots, and penning them into verses filled with vibrant imagery, intricate emotion, and carefully-crafted metaphor that turn them into works of art to enchant the reader. This is a book meant to be carried—into winding gardens, mountain trails, and quiet cafes—so bring it with you, savor each page, and let it inspire you to see the world as this poet sees it—full of wonder and beauty, even in the smallest flower blooming in the most unlikely place." — Rachel Clift, Author of *To Feel Anything At All*

"Kendall Hope invites you out on a walk with her in her latest book *The Willow Weepings*. It starts out as a frolic through beautiful fields of flowers, and then invites you into a cottage where she tells you, so personally, her feelings of heartbreak. Her beautiful words are enhanced by lovely photographs and illustrations. This is a very realistic journey of healing, and it was so well written." — John Queor, Author of *Resembling A Moth*

"*The Willow Weepings* is a stunning poetry collection that celebrates the glorious ecstasy and bittersweet agony that encompasses the totality of the human experience and honors Gaia's selfless gift of existing upon her gracious and sacred stage. Like the unfolding of vines and the unfurling of tender leaves and velvety petals, Hope weaves words and verses together into a sublime magic that pulses through the veins of the reader, soothing hearts in life's emotional flowing of seasons and rekindling the remembrance that we are all intimately linked to nature's cycles and that our very heartbeats are synced to the rhythm of her tides. *The Willow Weepings* is an unforgettable poetic experience that shouldn't be missed." — A. W. Jones, Author of *Mosaics of Shadow and Light*

"*The Willow Weepings* is an extraordinary collection of poetry that speaks to the inherent beauty that blossoms from observation of and connection with the natural world. Hope's words are a delightful mix of introspective knowledge and life-giving joy, accompanied by stunning photography and art. This poetry dances on the tongue and has never failed to make me smile." — Kristen Noelle Richards, Author of *as if to return myself to the sea*

"*The Willow Weepings* is a delicate collection that dives into the beauty of nature and the feelings of the heart. With each piece, Hope is weaving nature and emotion together into one entity, with beautiful illustrations and photographs to further emphasize the strength and fragility of the human experience." — Tiffiny Rose Allen, Author of *At The Beginning Of Yesterday*

"This is a beautiful love letter to nature, love, and loss. Through stunning imagery and snippets of memory and imagination, she portrays the rawness of heartbreak and the power of growth. These beautiful poems have been woven together with such emotional photography and charming illustrations. This poetry collection is a worthy successor to *Pockets of Lavender*, Hope's debut collection." — Madeleine S. Cargile, Starred Review

"This collection includes a delicious blend of poems that relax you, and others that leave you haunted. Coupled with gorgeous illustrations and photographs, Hope's work stays with you. Her poetry will inspire you to spend time outside appreciating nature as well as encouraging you to look inward even when it's painful." — Marlina Mossberg, Author of *Peach*

"This book puts a unique and idyllic lilt on oft-used motifs-and the abundant metaphors of nature are no low-hanging fruit in her capable hands. Like some of her Indie Earth peers, her poetry holds a timelessness and sincerity that much of contemporary poetry lacks. The book's compilation is ingeniously aware of itself. Even as it weeps, this collection wastes no time feeling sorry for itself in a beautiful world-dipping you into the mud only just long enough to show you that it too, is beautiful." — Jacquelynne Faith, Co-Creatix of the Sisterhood of Sacred Fire

"Merging the magic of fairytales and the wonder of nature together, *The Willow Weepings* takes your heart and soul into a journey where you dreamily get lost and found within Hope's poetry." — Annie Vazquez, Author of *My Little Prayer Book: Prayers, Poems, and Mantras for Illumination*

"Kendall Hope has crafted a book to devour in one sitting, only for you to return to and savor, with *The Willow Weepings*. Her poems hardly draw breath in their immediacy as she explores the emotional presence of heartbreak through the imagery of nature." — Renzo Del Castillo, Author of *Still*

"*The Willow Weepings* is a commentary on love, loss, and the process of grief. The collection navigates the grief process of letting go and finding new growth through free-form poetry, photography, and hand-drawn images. This personal and intimate collection invites the reader to a safe and whimsical space. I would recommend this read with a cozy cup of tea and a soft blanket." — Amy Harrison, Author of *healing: a collection of haiku*

"This book is full of so much wonder and beauty, especially for the smaller things in life. It is bursting with magic and hope. Hope writes in such a tender way that it just brings your imagination to life." — Jenna Nicole Stevens, Author of *Magic and Musings of the Universe: Love*

"I was impressed with the variety of poems in *The Willow Weepings*. You can tell that these are words that the author held closest to her heart and it was time to release them. The cover for this book itself pulls you in, but the black and white images, and emotions behind the poems get you to stay. I feel like this is a book that will help readers to feel safe and vulnerable in their feelings and emotions, while helping them to be strong at the same time." — J. A. Bishop, Author of *Her Colored Scars*

"A stunning collection of poems, Hope's words make the smallest things spectacular. She reminds us of the beauty in the world around as, and just how much a part of nature we are." — Heather Meatherall, Starred Review

*Disclaimer: Reviews have been edited for length and clarity.

The Willow Weepings

(poems)

Kendall Hope

Indie Earth Publishing Inc.
| Miami, FL |

The Willow Weepings

Kendall Hope

To any element of this earth,
to being human and part of nature.

To any human to ever exist,
to the soul, to the essence of being alive.

To love,
to being in love, being broken, and to the butterflies
that still come when the earth feels shattered.

To you.

A rainbow light, sprinkled with fairy dust
A Foreword by Flor Ana

In my time, I have read a vast array of books in a vast array of genres. But as I writer myself, I have always gravitated a little stronger towards fiction and poetry, and as I grew and developed my own voice as a writer, becoming a poet along the way, my love for the genre of poetry only grew exponentially stronger.

I had the honor of writing a foreword for Kendall's debut poetry collection, *Pockets of Lavender*, and I am honored to have been asked to write a foreword for Kendall's second collection, this book in your hands now, *The Willow Weepings*. In just the short time of a year, I have been able to see Kendall's tremendous growth as not only a writer, but as an artist, and it is seen, tasted, and felt in the pages you are about to embark on a journey with.

The Willow Weepings is a poetry collection like no other, written by a being who spreads magic upon all the beings she encounters and everything she touches. And in the time I have gotten to know her, to work with her, and help bring her books to fruition, I am glad to say that Kendall is not only an amazing person, but someone who has become a very good friend of mine despite the two thousand miles that keep us apart. In the two years I have known her, we have been able to laugh, cry, and connect on a level that is deep despite it all being via Zoom calls and text messages. This book will help you to see her through the eyes in which I view her: a talented young woman with the world ahead of her, with the ability to connect with nature and life itself in a way that exudes bliss.

As you board your reading of *The Willow Weepings*, know this poetry collection will make you feel. It will enlighten you with a love for nature that may have been laying dormant inside of you or further connect you to your synched breaths with the trees. It will allow you to view love in a new light, a warm bulb illuminating a room that may feel both confined and ever-expanding. It will touch your soul with the beautiful photographs Kendall has taken, the illustrations and characters she has created, and the purity and dedication in her heart to not only put this poetry collection together for herself, but for you as well, reader.

Kendall Hope is a ray of sunshine, a light beam that bends into a rainbow, leaving behind fairy dust that will make you feel a smile upon your face without you realizing it. Her poetry is a warm hand to hold, to adventure with as we dive into what makes us, us: our emotions and the nature we come from.

Table of Contents

The Willows... 1

Table of Contents

Table of Contents

Table of Contents

Table of Contents

Table of Contents

The Willow Weepings

Kendall Hope

The Willows

Ode to a Luna Moth

Oh, lovely Luna
You come from the moon
Only here a week
Soul purpose to seek
a beautiful mate.
Pale green searches the night
Silk in the sky
And when you meet the one,
you take further flight
until the day comes
when your soul must roam again.
How wonderful to have loved
until the very end.
Maybe not being able to stay forever
makes the love that much sweeter
and perhaps if you are born again,
you can find another love
with no end.

Lotus

The lotus grows of muddy water,
self-cleansing to keep pure
in its rebirth.
Gods and goddesses emerge and float,
the roots forgotten under murky layers.

September wildflowers & August honey

August honey, so sticky and sweet,
summer still cusps your tongue
not wanting to retreat.
Here, there are better sunsets you taste.
The start of the best part of the year,
the sun will soon greet Autumn with haste.

September wildflowers, warm and scattered.
Upon mountain towns,
the flowers blush from feeling flattered.
"We are here!" they wail as they will soon become frail.
Admired by the girl who kisses the bliss
of September wildflowers & August honey.

Weather spirit

I am the weather spirit.
I tend to match the sky and air.
I love a winter day
with a light cold surrounding.
Yet the sun touches my skin
and reminds me of who I am again.
My spirit tends to flow with the seasons
and I love feeling born again.
Sprouting and dying as the world goes round,
I am the weather spirit,
forever finding and releasing my ground.

Amber

I am trapped
like an ant
in amber resin
from the maple tree,
sticky and sweet,
encapsulating me,
as I wait for release.

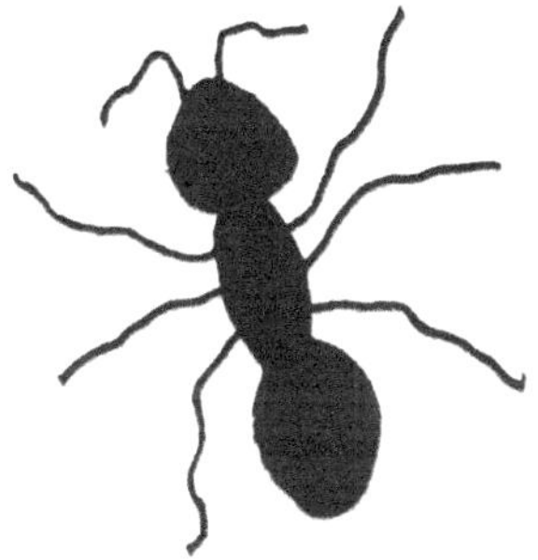

The aspens

It cannot be a coincidence,
the eyes of the aspen trees.
They see,
and their green hair turns gold
as the stories they've witnessed grow cold,
covered in a winter's new.
Some eyes seem to bleed.
What have they seen?
As I lay here and have a staring contest,
they win,
for they do not blink,
but I know that they think,
with the sky and the wind.
A shower of yellow,
that I lay in like a pillow.
A foreign but original language
as a chickadee hops among the tree,
yearning for the new season of rest.
The earth speaks to me
as I pause under the sunlit aspen trees.

Peeks of purple

Peeks of purple, still amongst the fall;
perhaps summer is not yet dead
after all.

                Cripple Creek

The creek cripples & ripples
                                Bent at the neck
                The sides disintegrating

        Fickle & broken

                Running still

                                Dry spell or
                                    monsoon

Chasing fireflies

Chasing fireflies
among the tall grass,
light in my eyes,
and my hands.
Lightning bugs
zap the summer's green.
In this yard,
I feel seen.

Hello, sweet earth

The grass waves hello
and rolls like the ocean
as the wind whispers among its tiny stems,
kissing small bugs hiding
among leaves and tufts.

MORPHO

Velvet wings of luster,
fluorescent and electric blue.
Delicate and feathered,
long lasting in this case for you to view.
To only live so long,
but to continue on in a glass frame.
In the gaze of my hazel eyes,
appreciating when it once flew the sky.

Flora & Fauna

Miss Flora and Fauna
start to compete
as emerald blades
glide under my feet.
Wildflowers bloom
and animals appear.
Isn't spring
just beautiful, my dear?

Fish in a cage

There is a vintage birdcage
that sits on a grandmother's dresser
with an interesting specimen inside.
A catfish in a bird cage.
Cat head, fish body.
A flounder with legs
it sometimes seems to be.
All turned around,
staring back at me.
This aquatic specimen,
does not need water, you see.
Whatever it is,
something is not quite right,
I am rather afraid
to sleep in its presence at night.

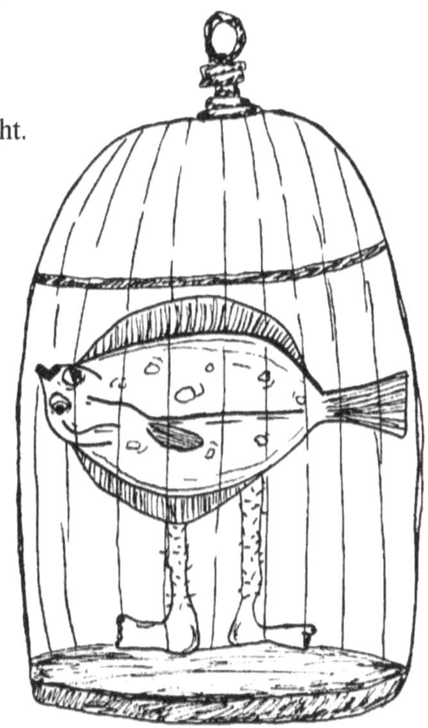

Peach

The velvet of the peach,
Wraps the bodice of the fruit,
With scuffed up marks,
That feel like lace.

Queen Anne's lace

Queen Anne's lace
rests upon the breast
of a queen suited for nature's king,
the flower,
a threaded beauty.

Wasps

I've never been stung
by a wasp.
Bees are my wholesome beings,
wasps the devil.
They prick,
a fiery sting,
no sweet honey for this mark,
sticky only with the needle of their anger.
DANGER!
Their eyes read in bright red,
right in the nerves.
Their stripes hypnotize
as they deceive the bees and devise
evil plans
with veils of anger.

Paper cicadas

You may know the chirp
of the cicadas,
sharp and loud.
But have you ever heard of the cicadas
that wear a paper crown?
Paper cicadas,
wings of papyrus,
their sounds in your head
becoming a virus.
Paper cicadas
dissolve into the night
when they are too tired
to rise and take flight.

The melted house

There is a melted house
across the street.
Rain on my window drips,
melting like candle wax
in view of the water.
The sky flames with sunset,
yet where is its wick?
Am I inside this candlestick?

Whittle some wood

Whittle some wood,
tittle the spout.
Tweedle dee, tweedle dumb,
go suck your thumb.
A splinter has got you,
and it's time to pout.

Big Dipper

The Big Dipper
is collecting the stars.
They seem so small to us,
yet our beings are smaller,
and we are the stars
that have deep and beautiful feelings,
hard and lovely,
as we float back one day
to the space of the sky.

The Big Dipper
collects us.
Three stars I notice on the handle—
our past, present, and future, perhaps.

Even on Earth,
you were my brightest star,
and you made me feel the most human.
Cup of stars,
here we are;
The Universe takes a sip
and the Big Dipper takes its dip.

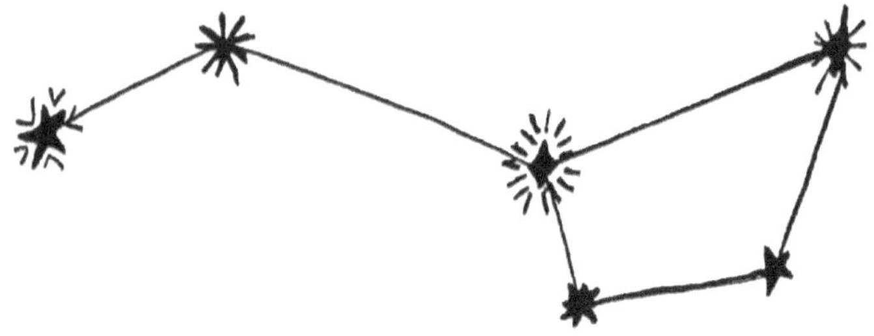

Dung beetle

Life is like the work of a dung beetle:
pushing shit,
but having beauty and a nature to fulfill,
noticing the world and taking your time
as you are on this forced-shit ride.
Crave the magic in the purpose and what you see along the way.
We are the dung beetle,
pushing through shit to see the beauty for another day.

Spider dew

Oh, to see the dew
on a spider web.
His home always there,
but the air doesn't seem to care
to make this home appear near
until it looks as though the spider's tears
are orbed among its strung up home.

String of pearls

String of pearls
across my neck.
Beaded plant
placed on my chest.
Nature's best accessory,
jewels of beaded chloroplast.
How I hope this necklace lasts.

Blue Hornworm

Maybe I am a blue hornworm,
like the one in Wonderland.
He inches and he crawls,
and if he doesn't die,
his wings sprawl
and he becomes a moth.

But, oh, the caterpillar state
is just as lovely.
He is my favorite color too,
a turquoise blue.
Stripes and patterned eyes,
horns of disguise.

You may think he is poisonous,
and he truly is in his natural state,
but maybe to some,
he is just what you want to taste.
Nightshade, deadly, would you like to try?
And though he is blue,
he does not always cry.

The busy bee's bottom

Submerged head first in a bell-shaped flower,
purple with power,
resting and working behind a young lady
writing in the grass,
the busy bee's bottom is buzzy indeed.

Roly poly

Swallow the pill bug.

Here he comes,

He eats the decay.

Small and curious.

I love how he plays.

And to you, it is just another day.

Roly poly,

Pill bug so dry,

Can he give you a hug?

Makes me cry.

Miss peregrine falcon

Oh, Miss peregrine falcon,
what do you see
as you soar the gloomed sky
over me?

Moondrops

Moondrops in the jar,
I drink them from a vile.
Magic glistens in my blood,
Candied sugar plum dreams,
sandman gleams
on cobblestone streets.

Petrichor

The perfume of the earth.
Once it has released its breath
from the fresh shower it has taken,
scents whir to your nose.
How kind that it shares this garnish
of dew on the earth's hue.

KILLING
FOR
CONSERVATION

The old moth that lived in a shoe

There was an old moth that lived in a shoe,
chewed a hole through the toe of the boot,
the porch light an aglet that glows in the dark,
the light in the closet, only here to be found.

The moth likes to keep busy;
in the day, she makes pies.
The moth does not fall sleepy
and at night, she roams the skies.
She makes a candlelight dinner
with the match she has found;
warm wings and a few bug friends gathered around.

The moth lives peacefully in her shoe…

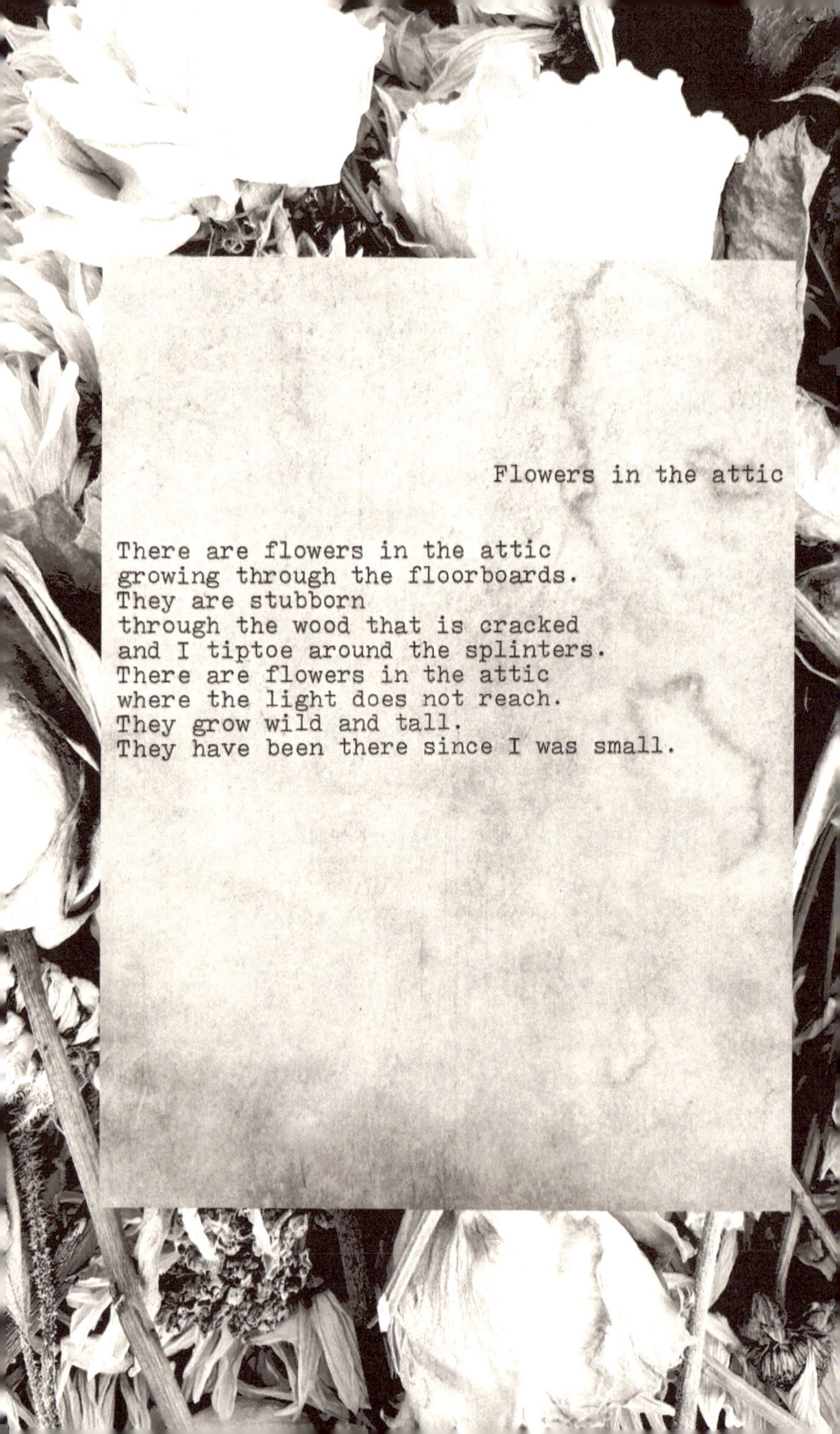

Flowers in the attic

There are flowers in the attic
growing through the floorboards.
They are stubborn
through the wood that is cracked
and I tiptoe around the splinters.
There are flowers in the attic
where the light does not reach.
They grow wild and tall.
They have been there since I was small.

My little cottage

I imagine, almost daily,
of my little cottage.

The one with the pretty purple flowers
and no view of cell phone towers.

The one with a path of moss
that leads to a yellow art shed.

I dance with my garden
and paint among the woods.

I throw myself tea parties in the forest,
for it is my backyard,
and I can make any day feel grand.

The sun shines just right into my windows,
through suncatchers and stained glass.

And on rainy days,
I would love my little cottage, too,
for my sky there
mustn't always appear baby blue.

I dream of my little cottage,
almost every day.
And I believe I shall make it happen
and still have room for play.

Cornflower blue

Cornflower blue,
what a pretty hue.
No yellow present,
no corn resemblance.
Known as invasive,
one of my favorites.
Beautiful and true,
only spreading its beauty to you.
Native to its land,
cornflower blue.

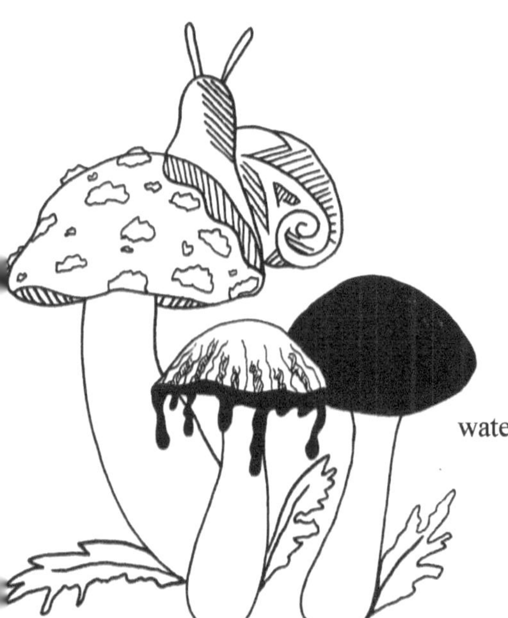

Ink cap tears

Watch the ink cap
bleed its silky black tears
into blue veins
over the years
as mycelium holds hands
below the surface,
watered from the ink cap's pain.

Lilacs, lavender, and lemons.

I hope you feast over the
thoughts,
smells,
and tastes
of the rich
lilacs,
lavender,
and lemons
that have been with you all along.

And may you suckle upon their grasp
of gentleness and fruitful fertility
for the mind.

Pocket posies

Pocket full of posies,
cheeks so red and rosy.
Giggle, giggle as I fall
down,
      down,
           down.
Into a pile of leaves,
I drown.

Pocket full of posies,
dandelions among my toesies.
Make a wish and a fairy is born,
and she spins, spins, spins,
amongst the gentle kisses of the

W
  I
    N
      D,

carrying strands of my curls into whisps among freckles.
Sparkles adorn my hazel brown.

Pocket full of posies,
feeling fairly cozy.
In a moment for only smiles
there is no room for

    O W
  R   N
F   S.

Moss in my pockets

There are crumbs of moss
in my pockets
and leaves in my hair,
mud on my shoes
and salt in the air.

A day well spent.

I miss the ocean

I miss the ocean.
She is rather lovely,
and I am sad I cannot say hello,
but maybe she misses me.

I saw her for the first time ever,
and you were there.
And now, when you no longer are,
she is still there,
and she always will be,
calling to me when I need.

She flows on,
even if we just become stories
from walking on her beaches.
She sees many come and go,
but she is there forever,
stuck in her flow.
And, one day, I will come back to her
and say hello.

Pickle jar of flowers

She sets her pickle jar of flowers
on her windowsill of rainbows.
Lily's aroma permeates the air
and tickles the sweet girl's nose.
A fly buzzes by
without a care.
Glass that is reused for something
beautiful and new.
A pickle jar of flowers
just might surprise you.

Mellow yellow

Breathe in the aspens today

& they'll melt your troubles away.

Soon, they will turn yellow

& maybe your brain
can feel more mellow.

Sea grass

Sea grass on rocks,
ebbing in the water like hair.
Mother Nature's human elements are everywhere.
In the water, untangled and flowing,
out of water, green and glowing.
Rocks so jagged, little biomes grow.
Oh, let my sea grass hair flow,
in the river, among the shore.
Let me rest evermore.

The cricket chirps

The cricket chirps,
rubbing its legs
like I do in bed
after a fresh shave.

Rubbing our feet together,
a warm and gentle caress,
socks making static
as we chirp sweet sleepy sounds.

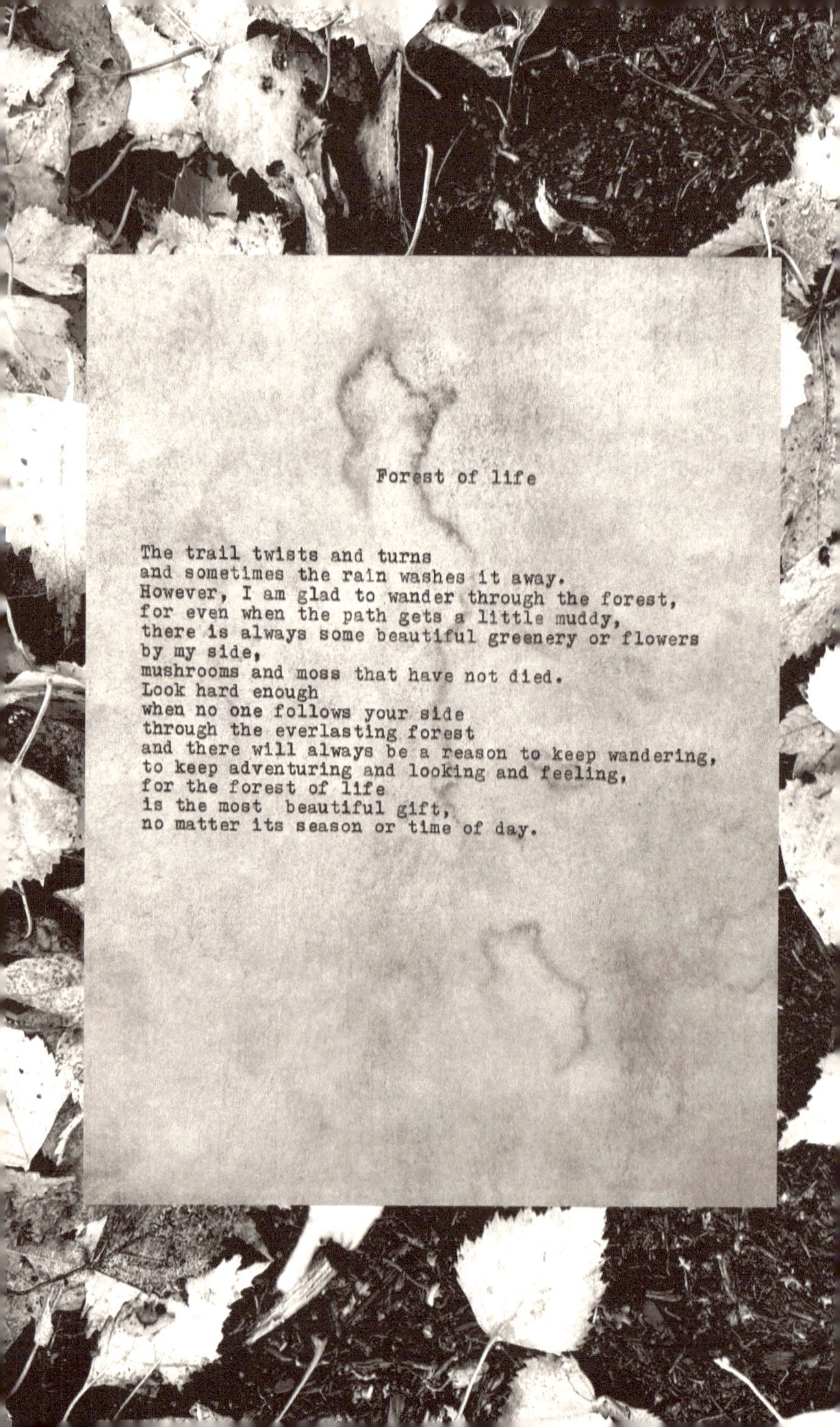
Forest of life

The trail twists and turns
and sometimes the rain washes it away.
However, I am glad to wander through the forest,
for even when the path gets a little muddy,
there is always some beautiful greenery or flowers
by my side,
mushrooms and moss that have not died.
Look hard enough
when no one follows your side
through the everlasting forest
and there will always be a reason to keep wandering,
to keep adventuring and looking and feeling,
for the forest of life
is the most beautiful gift,
no matter its season or time of day.

Tiny green grasshopper

Tiny green grasshopper,
hopping out of the bindweed flowers.
They close up into a warm pink,
have tangled vines and do not stink.
The water they drink makes them grow lush.

This tiny green grasshopper is in a rush.
The itsy bitsy guy,
as small as a fly,
hops in the blink of an eye.

Faeries

I think I like bugs so much
because maybe they are faeries.
They do not necessarily have to hide,
and so when you see one,
maybe let it be,
for if I were a fairy,
a bug I think I would be.

Barefoot

Raw, feeling the earth.
Grounded, how I'm meant.
Feet are the channel to all.
I watch my wet prints follow,
like I am a child looking behind my shadow,
planting my feet into the earth,
into grass, water, dirt.
Feet.

Firefly in the storm

Oh, little firefly,
look at how the sky cries.
Your wings will not have time to dry
if you race through the storm.
Sit in the bellow of thunder
and wait for the clouds to pass.
You have been glowing this whole time
and eyes notice you in the night.
When the sun shines again,
you can take your own flight.

Dandelion

Stems coiling in water
Leaking white to stick to my fingers
Bleeding yellow smushed on the ground
Dried into my tea
Purple leads into green
Hairs like my legs
Creamy and new
Yellow hugs the environment
for the bugs that roam
A thriving ecosystem
soon to turn into puffs
Fairies are born
Dancing through the wind
Spreading their seeds once more
for the dandelions in next year's store

The lips of the flowers

Acacia and magnolia
meet in the park
just as the world mellows
and the sky grows dark.
The lips of these flowers
start to part,
and under the moon,
there is the start of a spark.

Owl

An owl so wise
talks to the night
with only a calm and invisible presence,
knowing *hoo* and who not is in the woods.
But if you look closely,
you might see those wide eyes glimmer
as its head spins towards you,
gazing and listening
among a branch of pine
that splinters but doesn't hurt,
for the owl is strong.

Bumble

I saw the first bee of the season.
He was crawling,
and I was too distant to get him sugar water.
I hope he made it far,
for I saw the first bee of the season
and I cannot wait to see more.

Mantis

What does the mantis think
as he peers at you
through his wise and tiny eyes?
Do you stare back at him,
knowing you wear a disguise?
Does he prey upon your insecurities,
or does he pray for that hidden personality?

Bugs on my wall

I have
bugs on my wall,
ones that don't crawl,
ones I appreciate
and stare at delicately.
Perfectly crisp,
their souls a whisp,
I have
bugs on my wall.

Inker tinkle little stinkle

Oh, little stink bug, taking on its own world,
the first big bug I've seen of spring.
You spray your enemies with disgust and no remorse.
In return, they squish on you til your guts grow green
and rust the sidewalk.
Yet, spring has sprung,
and more bugs will come.

Snapdragons

Snapdragons from your grandmother's garden,
flowers like tissue paper,
amaranth that hangs,
pollen falling on my bedside table,
making it troubling with my nose and breath.
Do not mind the amaranth.
Wanting to dry and preserve their glory,
but knowing I can also let them be a part of my story.
Left untouched
as they wither away
and spread all dry
on the ground of a summer's day.

Wild berries and mums

Wild berries and mums;
through the candle, the smells hum,
You read in your green chair
as you age with silver hair;
Autumn is here, my dear, &
the leaves turn yellow amongst your window.
Read of magical worlds in your novels,
yet do not forget how magical your own world follows.

Frost

I like when I remember to appreciate the cold.
I see frost on twigs from the dead trees of the season.
I always know it's there when the cold days come.
But sometimes,
you just need to remember the beauty of the water,
not just melted,
but crystalized and formed,
overlooked,
fragile and easily gone,
but created with such strong bond.
I like to remember the frost
that the cold brings.
It's one of those things
not forgotten entirely
but that needs to be refreshed.

The Weepings

                    The Willow Weepings

I want to cry to the forest
& weep with the willows.
I want to scream to them,
for I know they can hear me.
I want them to speak to me,
yet all they do is stare.

You say they are just trees
and I say you are wrong.
I know that the willows that weep
crave love that is deep
and they are forever cursed
with their lips pursed
from crying for hours on end.
Where do I stop
and they begin?

I knew love

I knew love.
True love.
That's no doubt,
and it will never the removed from my mind
because no matter,
the better or worse that comes for me now,
I knew love.
And therefore,
I know love
and all that it can be
and is.
I am love.

I knew love,
and even if the fears are real
and I never find it again
and it will never be in the same exact way,
how fantastic is it
that I have known and felt love
as love should be?
Love, love, love…
Love me.

Almond Eyes

She had….

almond shaped eyes
with a dilated gaze,
of amaretto chocolate irises.

Cupid's bow, a cherry taste,
with a hint of sweet cashew lips,
the curve just enough,
Salty to the taste
like sips from the ocean.

Oh, golden sun

Oh, sun-setting golden hour,
fogged up car glass,
kissing ink and lips ever so,
eyes gazing and hair grazing with gentle and passionate hands.
The sun all around,
its memory to always last.

How lucky I am to see
such a beautiful being in this fading, yet bold, sunlight.

Geese in the field watching our souls dance.
One last time, but never our last chance.
Alas they fly right above our eyes
after we have watched the sunset,
blanket wrapped tight
as the warmth of the sky fades away
into a Cheshire Cat smile moon.

The symbol of closure,
and yet our hearts forever last.
This is new, my dear,
and though it's fragile now,
it has been and will always be
a wonderful past.

Here is to the future,
a new day of sunshine
while this moment is encapsulated
in every foreseen sunset.

Let us leave it in a memory,
a golden orb of love in my mind.

Heartbreak

I always thought
I would die of heartbreak.
I thought I would be old
& die from the heartbreak of
the one I love's death.

But I'm still so young
and this heartbreak makes me think
I might just die.

I just might.

Guts gone green

My guts have gone green,
queasy in my death,
mossy and thick,
my insides encapsulated,
flourished & fresh.

Fuck

Only sad,
crying to the brim,
surface tension on the tea cup,
I think I'll cry forever.

Fuck.

Now I'm mad,
I hate being mad,
the tension broken,
the tea spilled.

Fuck.

It comes in waves,
I did not think I would break this way,
I guess it's a new day,
stages of grief.

Fuck.

Swept out from under my feet,
now I slip,
no running by the pool,
only diving and drowning.

Fuck.

Wipe away that frown.

                                        Sonder

I go about my day
passing or thinking of strangers,
reaching sonder of another
as they live their own lives.

Breathing their own air,
seeing their own beauties,
feeling their own range of emotions,
being their own person,
lacking or flourishing in their own love,
struggling with their own pains,
creating their own memories,
visiting their own places.

I have been there too.
Lives seen only
in glimpses.

Snowdrops & Forget-Me-Nots

You've left me among the Winter,
the hardest season of my being.
And I sit here and wonder
if the forget-me-nots have withered in your mind.
Even after all the promises
of the white clovers,
you left me lonely and broken,
and you seem to be unphased.
Leaving me untended,
to mend myself as I watch.
And in this Winter,
there grows a new flower.
Here bloom the snowdrops,
for new beginnings and hope.
I am full of hope, as you should know,
so I think now I must listen to these blossoms
and grow.
New roots to come
from the new sun of my heart.
My sunshine has left,
yet I won't stay stranded in the dark.

House blue jitters

Life often beats you up all at once,
yet you resolve, rise, and continue,
singing your tune.

Raspberries

The raspberries bleed
and my teeth feel the seeds
stuck in my craters
and the pain runs deep.

The devil that's sweet

An angel and devil sit on my shoulders,
deviled eggs hatch tiny beasts,
though this one is a little bit sweet—
not too bitter, but ask the angel.
She has a bit of sass.
Sitting here, they spiral and clash—
a little bit of good and evil.

Alice in her bottle

Tears becoming a sea,
How much of these waters can be released from me?
Now I am surrounded and cannot leave.
To ever stop crying,
seems it simply cannot be.
A purgatory of a dream.
This wonderland,
beautiful, but so sad.
Singing in the rain of my tears,
Face hot and my screams fogging the glass.

Cling

Clung to you like eggs on a leaf.
Easy to crush
by the fingers of a human.

Stuck on strong,
when the forces of wind,
rain, or sun,
try to break me away from you.

And it was your fingers,
who simply seemed
to pinch me off,
as I was clinging for life
and growth alongside you.

But I guess, after all,
a breath that is clung,
will run out of air
eventually.

Green cardigan

You hung me up,
like that favorite green cardigan
I loved to see you wear.

Left to dry in the sun
on a cloudy day.

Ectoplasm

Forest of fog.
Ghostly residue
on my heart.
Twisted tendrils of branches,
caging my love.
The ghost of a lover
passing through.

Looking glass

Staring in the looking glass,
years of reflection
look back at me.
Reflection has been watching me
or I have watched myself,
growing,
aging,
moving,
being.
Looking back at me,

                    myself,

                            through the looking glass

Kendall Hope

Venus flytrap

Are there flies on Venus?
The plant swallows the planet.
Venus is born.
Swallow her whole
and alive.
Wings clipped in the teeth of miss Venus,
crumpled and black, she curls
when her anger unfurls
and kills herself internally.
Take me to that planet
and let me float away.

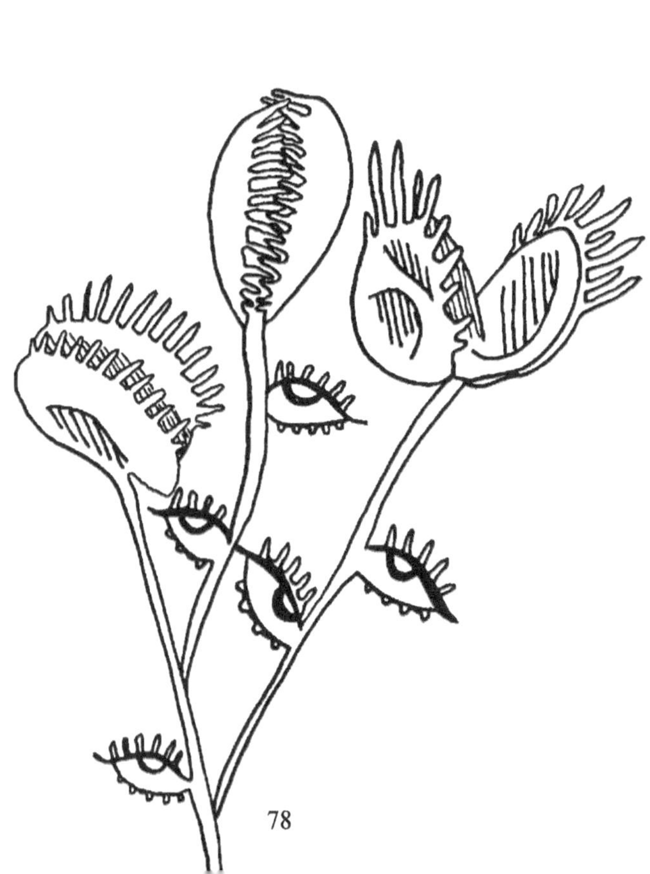

Seasons you came

4 of each season,
4 seasons there are.
Is that all that could last?
Summer, spring, fall, winter
repeated 4 times
before you had to melt like the snow,
fade like the leaves
and let me go?
Each of those seasons were the best I've ever seen;
I guess now
the seasons are up to me
and maybe a little less serene.

Forget forget forget

I do not want to forget.
How could I?
I can not,
but what if…
What if we made it?
What if it happens?
What if all that held back heals?
What if, what if, what if…
Please, please, please,
do not let me forget.
How can I force
away, away, away
these feelings I've been so devoted to
Every. Single. Day?
How can I?
It is impossible to ever nearly stop.
But please,
keep me here
and never leave.
Please, please, please,
my heart might need to move on,
but please,
let the memories in my head stay strong.

Loves me not

He loves me,
    He loves me not

        I love him,
          I love him not.

I love him, though,
    And always will
      Always
        When he does not
          With every last petal
           Picked off the stem

            I'll love him more
            Even without him

Salt of the slug

Spill the salt.
But it isn't good luck?
Burns the body
of the slug.
A grain stings your eye
and creates a sty.
Is that why you are so blind?
Truly can't see with your eyes
and what's meant to be,
so I am here, left behind.

Honeybody

Oh, honeybody,
sticky with golden bees,
skin made of honey and glass.
Ginkgo leaves fall from the trees
and dance in front of your warmth,
kiss your freckles
and my lips cannot release
from your honeybody.

PAINted sky

When we are pained,
we tend to speak or look or reach to the sky.
For who, or what, or why,
we may not know.
Yet something above our heads
and the cosmic vibrations pull my eyes
to everlasting skies.

An array of clouds on azure,
orange whipped with pink hues.
Or stars against a deep black blue,
the same way my heart is bruised.

Fog on the resting edge of a pale breath,
pain seems to slowly release
as I melt my way up
against gravity
and release my soul
into the pain-tinted sky.

Making wishes

I'm still wishing on eyelashes
and keeping pinky promises,
though they don't mean the same to you.
Maybe, in another universe,
there's an us that's better.
I don't want to think of one that is worse,
and if there is,
then this is the best,
though I'm not sure I feel that in my chest,
but maybe in the rest,
we make it in the way we imagine.
We have to be connected to our dreams, in a reality somewhere.
Why can't it be here?

Feelings

Do you think the moon and the sun have feelings?
That the moon may cry when the sun says goodbye?
Do you think the grass has feelings?
That it tickles you when it feels your presence
to acknowledge your love for its soil?
Do you think the clouds have feelings?
That they breathe in and out and reach
for one another in an embrace?
Do you think the trees have feelings?
That they speak to each other underground
and cry when they forget their roots?
Do you think that your feelings are enough?
Just as enough as anything in the whole world could have?
They are all worthy.
And the best part
is that you are a human
and those feelings are meant to be.

Poems of you

I write poems of you
and all out of love,
even the heartbreak ones,
because, when push comes to shove,
you were MY love,
and that never changes,
though the stars have rearranged.

I loved you, my dear,
and I always will.
So how does it feel
to be my muse still?
To have poems of you,
and you know who you are,
because after all,
you were my shooting star.

Here for a bit,
gone in a flash it seems,
comparatively
to the life of our dreams.

Quilt

If my life is a quilt
and I am sewing up the patches,
I think, in the end,
when my days are finished,
the patch made up of you
will be one of my favorites,
one of the most beautiful.

Colors and warmth and textures,
all on one square
that I look at forever
until the very last day,
where I shall lay under my quilt
when it is time to decay.

Trinkets

Trinkets sit on my bookshelf,
some packed away,
ready to be displayed
in a beautiful home one day.
A cottage in the forest
with a garden on the side.
An art shed painted yellow
where I can paint and watch the sky.
A corner to read and write
and windows to feel the sunlight.

Trinkets sit on my bookshelf,
now and in my dream home
and I take it one day at a time.
Curiosities, books, and thingamabobs lined,
all unique to me
and what makes me feel alive.
I think I like my things
because they are symbols of me,
so take a look around my room,
learn from its museum and see.

Bookstore floors

I would like to sit on bookstore floors with you,
as we do *(did)*,
and scrunch my nose at you,
and give you a laugh or two,
and hold your face,
while we slow down our pace
and sit on bookstore floors.

Hello lovely...

Hello lovely... How are you really?
Take a cry on my shoulder,
it will not hurt you.
Let it all out, for spring is near.
Each season, darling,
I'm here.

Break the spell

Break the spell,
for my heart swells.
Painful force to unlove,
and I never meant to enchant.
We were meant to be.
If the spell must be broken,
please do not sip the poison.
It hurts too much,
and my blood is already drained
and filled with spiders
that make me jitter with anger and fear.
Is there a spell for heartbreak?
This heart feels so bleak,
it hurts to speak.
Nausea and hypnosis,
never going anywhere
because your name is set in stone
in the grave of my mind
and I visit you every day.
Must I beg for responses?
Or were you already dead
when you didn't reassure
the cockroaches in my head.

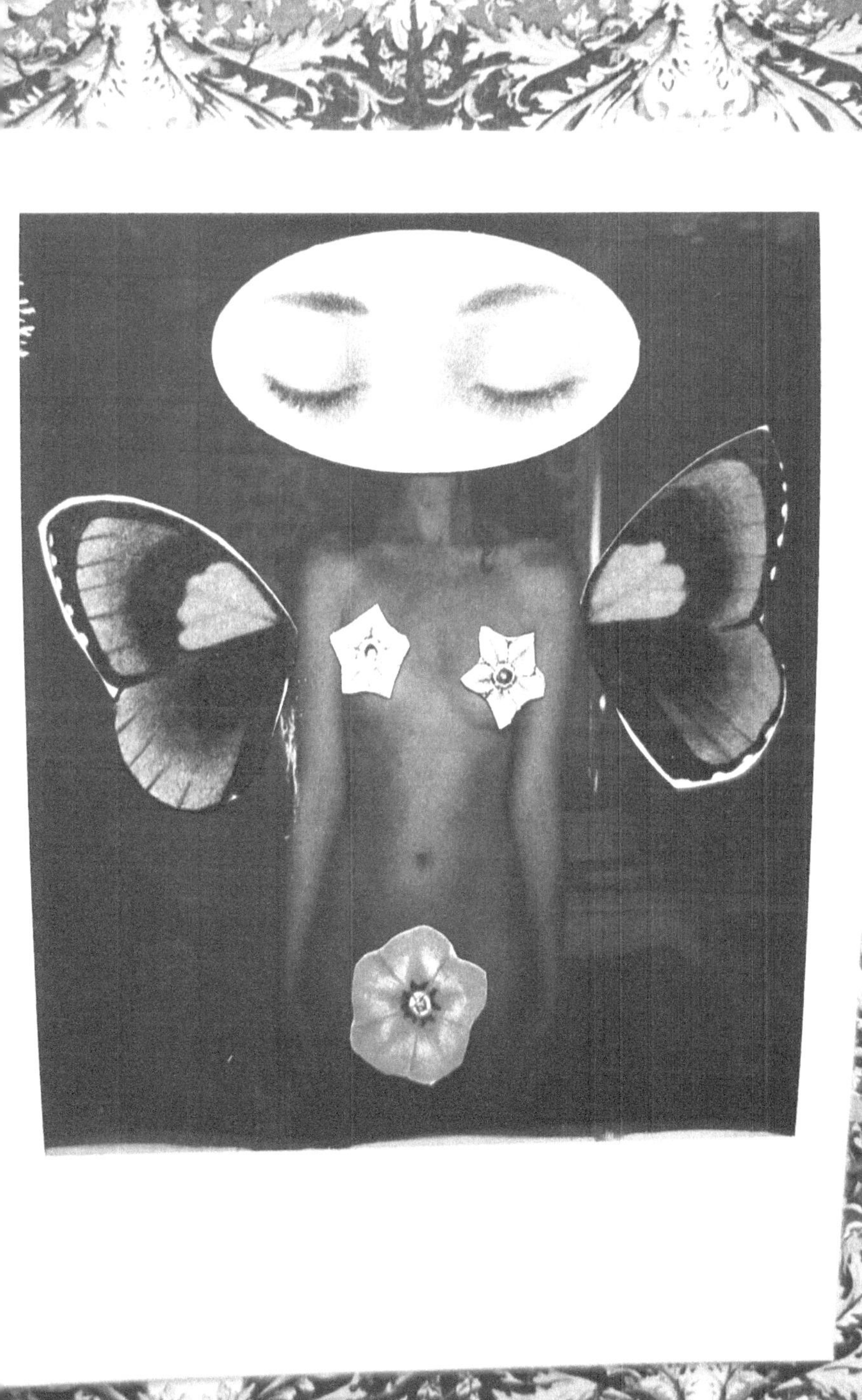

Forever

I know I was more than enough
and that I am not replaceable.
The personal touches still stay
and I know I'm the one that got away.

But I fear, my dear,
that your fears
are what kept you from keeping me.
And if you give yourself to someone else one day,
I'll know I wasn't enough for you
to break your fears.

Something that I can no longer provide,
I hope you give to yourself kindness.
Please, be kind.
Your well-being will never escape my mind.

Every day giving everything I could,
I still couldn't break the spell.
And after years,
I couldn't find the antidote
for you to keep me.

Someday morning

Someday morning, maybe you'll bring me my favorite things
and confess a love for me
that never went away,
and that you'd like to start again today
and never let it fade away.
Never.
Someday morning.
Perhaps, never mourning.

Pain

Maybe it's okay that the pain lasts so long.

Perhaps, I know that it meant something deep.

Cooked

Lying in this hot bath,
I'm cooked.
Might as well add some veggies.
Make me a stew;
it's hot enough
to feel something
and avoid shivers—
my mind already deals with those
bubbles added.
I boil,
I sweat and I cry.
Will I taste too sweet or salty for this medley?
Who knows.
I don't know if you'll ever want to taste me again;
lips to the ladle
and it burns,
and somehow,
the words don't hurt as much
as the face that you make,
avoiding me
in distaste,
letting me simmer here,
wondering if one day again
you'll love me in the way you did.
As I cool in the body,
I'm tired of being left here to soak,
left to feel
the lack of you.

Silver

Long hair of silver,
sweet as silk from the silkworm,
sweet as the sound of the harpsichord
as her hands run through.
Some parts wirey,
some parts gold.
Oh, what sweet whispers
has this hair been told
as the lady beneath it
has grown old?

Rainy town

Me and my lover,
encapsulated in the most lovely hotel room.
We do not own the place,
but the night is still ours.
Opening the window
to hard windy rain,
the direction passes by,
not touching our window frame.
I look at the lights and blurs,
tipsy and relaxed.
We listen, we observe.
I could stay in this memory for hours.
Overlooking the town's street,
our love towers.
We listen and we look,
as our eyes and street lights glisten.
This moment is real,
with nothing left, but to feel.

                        After sun

A fter the sun
  has gone away,
a new moon
  has come for my new days.
I am not so sure
  if the sun has fully left me,
but I do know
  that the moon is helping me gently.

Heart

My heart has kept me going
For every single
bloody second my life has had.
From the very beginning,
it has not stopped,
even when it has broken.
Heart strings snapped,
it has kept going
and kept me alive.
The brain teases it sometimes
for how hard I love,
but I am glad my heart has been here
beating for every tear
that fills my eyes blind.

Miss Lana

I wish to be like Miss Lana when I grow old.
Stories of her artist friend beautifully told,
glasses that rest along her nose
as a dusty chain connects to her clothes.
Eyes blue and soul that shines through,
clips full of gray hair strung above her crown.

The guiding hand and heart,
they lead me here.
And how beautiful it is
to hold this woman—
practically a stranger—
so dear.
Saturated beauty to the eyes,
I am every age in here.
A representation of my insides
resides in this blue corner building.

Magic and beauty strung around,
pure art and humanity around these rooms.
A gentle yet tight hug goodbye,
forever singing its tune
in my mind with the works of Rockey
to hang in my home on gallery walls to stare.

Magical.
An interaction spontaneous and connected.
We flourish being human, and living full of new perspectives.

Mismatched reading chairs

Oh, mismatched reading chairs,
that would have been.
We would have held hands
and maybe kissed as we read.
Lost in fantasy worlds,
but next to each other.
I guess my reading chair
sits alone from another.
So I sit and I read
and think of what could be,
but at least
I have a chair for me.

The tears won't roll

The tears won't roll,
won't ebb and flow.
They stay bubbled inside,
and it's not due to my pride.
I want to cry.
And cry.
And cry.
Oh, but do not pry.
It will leak when it wants.
Untamed, it haunts.
A weep full enough,
for you cannot always be tough.

Summertime sadness

Summertime sadness, they say.
How has it lingered into my days?

I thrive off of sunshine,
so why is my mind deciding to be unkind?

To keep me still when I wish to explore.
I thought this sadness was for the season next door.

The winter holds my seasonal depression,
so, why now, must you begin?

Cold tongued

I have noticed my tongue has gone cold.
Not with words,
but it feels cool,
like ice in my mouth.
Is it because of the lack of yours
entangled with mine?
A fire missing,
burnt out.
Please light the spark,
so we may start again.

Man on the moon

Man on the moon,

Do your feet stay grounded?
I float up to you,
the gravity of you,
on the moon.

But you are too far out of reach,
and even the draw of gravity on Earth
cannot pull you to me.

Man on the moon,
a fantasy now.
The stars must rock me to sleep,
because they are the dust that make up my bones.
I am my new home.
You said you'd watch me forever,
but you seem more distant than Saturn.

Maybe one day,
I can wish upon the moon again,
when it is less blue.

Love letters

I cannot sleep
and I begin to weep.
Songs all of you,
brain all on you,
love letters in my desk
kept neat and nice,
only to be letters of being loved.
What now am I to love?
I never thought there would be an after.
I thought you were my happily ever.
That's all.
I think of your words,
and now, I can no longer wait on them,
and I cannot even hear your voice
or have your presence as I sleep.
I am only meant to miss you.
Nothing more.
But still,
I lie here
and I cry,
and I think of what *should* have been,
what *would* have been
and was going to be.
And now,
it is only what *could* have been.

One day

I keep thinking of one day.
One day again in plenty of ways,
one day where you'll have me again.
Because I will never fall out of love,
and someday,
when it's just right,
one day,
when I'll be here,
you will look at me the way you did,
as we grew and we loved,
and we can one day,
one day,
have it again.

Sun-kissed orange

She paints her nails sun-kissed orange,
frames art on her walls
and allows sleepy eyes to take her over.

Her sunny room radiates warmth
and dreams of clementines kissing her cheeks;
an afternoon nap
with sun-kissed nails.

In the dead of winter,
even in the midst of
feeling her crushed melancholic soul,
she is a touch of summer.

Skeleton in the snow

Will my bones grow cold?
No skin to shiver.
No goosebumps quiver.
No heart to grow fatigued and freeze.
Skeleton in the snow,
might I be old?
Have I been buried by blizzards?
Garden sow,
use my bones to hold upright flowers.
Winter shall pass,
and I shall shine again.

                              Roots

I want to die and be turned into a tree
with you buried next to me.
Our roots holding hands,
branches whispering sweet words into the wind.
And here with you,
I am me.
You know me.

But even as I die and become a tree,
only I know truly what it means to be me.
S o try your best,
be as kind as you can.
Those in life will snap your branches from time to time,
or let you wither in seasons passing.

But now as a tree,
you are here,
and I am me.
How lovely it is to be a tree.

April fools

I think my heart was left in April
on the cold Pacific coast
where time froze and everything felt just right,
where neither loved each other most,
preserved in perfect memories since that week.

I felt truly happy.
All was perfect.
April changed forever,
'Twas my absolute favorite adventure.
No second passed that I don't remember.

Am I now a fool?
Have I been one since that April?
She will come again,
yet never the same
as that true beautiful week in my head,
frigid in my brain's ice box
where nothing can crack the feelings.

You were my April fool,
down to the day.
Thread falls off the spool,
blue thread runs out,
and I prick my finger.
You are sewn into my head,
and now, only patchwork.
I keep the quilt of our memories warm
against this new raging cold.

I felt like I was fully alive,
and I feel it each time I reflect.
Oh, I love that April trip.

Here I go,

T
  i
    p...
      T
       i
        p...
          D
          r
          i
          p.

Am I a fool
to think of that April
and loving you?
No, we were never a joke.
I feel only a fool now that I cannot have you in the next,
like that sweet April
where everything was complete.

Once you have met her

Once you have met her
and have heard what she has to say,
a tickle will reminisce in your mind
from time to time.
Not always in your head crystal clear,
but a lingering sunshine ray,
she is perhaps a person not easy to find,
and for her, you might not stay,
But once you have met her,
a bit of sunshine is forever in your days.

Rainbow

Her essence is…

Red like the skin of an apple
in the hot July sun.
Orange like the sun while it sets
and lemonade hits my tongue.
Yellow like the honey
that comes from the sweetness of the bees.
Green like the bruises that grow old
from sitting in dirt on my knees.
Blue like the water that comes from
the sky and cerulean sea.
Purple like the fields of lavender
that release a pleasant scent with the breeze.

She is as raw as a rainbow.

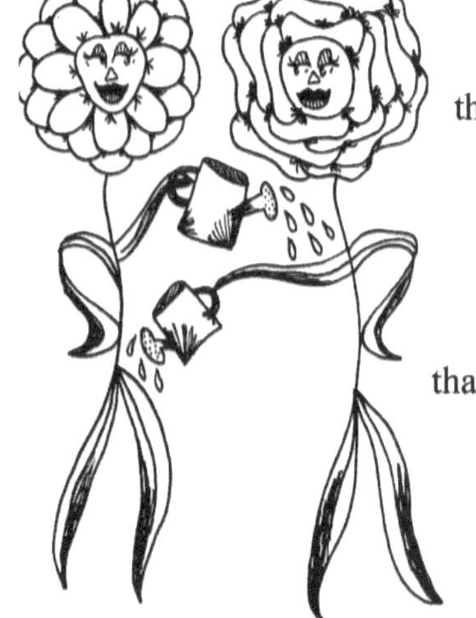

Chrysalism

Calm in the chrysalis of my home's chest,
feeling tranquil while it thunders,
reaching only through my rounded window.
The shutters shiver with the rain jitter
and I am in my iridescent dream.
The sun may not be gleaming,
but here I am safe,
as the god of weather
allows the thunder to rattle my bones
and soothe my restless body.

All the bright places

Do you ever look at things
and see how full it seems?
The color is literally lack of saturation;
it messes with you.

Where is the color?
Where is the brightness?
I think of you
and all the bright places,
and mostly, it's images
of your face,
or mine,
in the sunshine.

Of course, one likes a glum day—
we need them after all—
but, man, oh man,
I like the bright ones.

Why, as you get older,
the colors literally grow dull?
I LOVE seeing color
and I like to imagine
all the bright places.

You're like a rainbow,
the spectrum of color
all reflecting
into my eyes,
more incredible than just a rainbow.

I gave you flowers

I gave you flowers.
No one gives boys flowers.
You took them kindly,
& I received some from you too,
but eventually, they stopped.
I kept them dried in a box.
Even with the death of them,
I remembered the beauty they brought
as you came into my life,
never to be gone again.
I do not get those flowers any longer,
so now I shall keep planting my own.
These flowers will grow stronger,
they come from my veins
as I whisper to my plants
and to myself inevitably,
"Good job growin,' keep on goin.'"

Stars and Moons

You couldn't give me the stars,
when I gave you the universe.
Helping someone else reach the moon,
but where were you for me?
Where are you,
when I'm still a shining sun?
You don't even know
the depths of the cosmos I would go—
and went, for that matter—
for you,
but thanks for *(not)* asking anyways
how my world has been…

Wishing well

Today, I feel close to you.
I do not know what tomorrow entails.
However,
I cannot keep waiting for you
at the wishing well.

Taste my skin

Vanilla bean paste makes up my freckles.
My rosy cheeks taste of pomegranate.
My scars taste of ecstasy.
Or is that wrong?
For I want to taste real.

My scabs taste of the blood of a tomato.
Bitter, but better when mixed with the crust of my pale skin.
Doughy in the middle and crisp from the sun.
Feel my peach fuzz amongst your lips.

My skin calls to be tasted
of the many flavors
this body offers.

The Candlelight Ghost

I watch a candlelight ghost
float
down the hall, across my bed.
Is she finding a place to rest her head?
Of translucent & flowy hair,
covered in rags,
I see her breath escape the lungs she once had,
now only a willow of a wisp, cold & crisp

Kendall Hope

The Tortoise and The Hare

Ahead, ahead,
I know who I am.
I know what I want.
THERE IS THE FINISH LINE
oh no, my foot is caught.

Left behind, behind,
for you to learn and gain your wisdom.
Slow pace,
will you win the race?

It was never a competition.
I was holding your hand the entire ride
and I took my steady time.
Believe me.
Waiting, waiting, time was ticking,
ever so slow.
I learned to grow.
We're late, we're late,
for this very important date.

But now, I must wait some more,
for you to reach the shore.
Crashing waves.
There is the finish line,
among the tides.

Ahead in the head,
Behind in the time.

Maybe one day, this tortoise and hare
can meet together again
at the finish line.

Crow confetti

My collection of treasures,
my most precious gem.

No longer mine.

Lost from my pile,
but not because I was careless.

Not because I didn't keep track.

A button grew legs
and walked away from me.

No longer mine.
No longer mine.

I force myself to not seek my lost thing.

It no longer wants to be mine.
Most precious thing is myself.

It's nothing I can find on the floor or in store.
I cannot find my button
even with the call of its name.

Withered

I am withered, but not broken.
I have the crinkled wings of a butterfly,
with wiggly antenna still reaching for the sky.
I will rehydrate, and once again dry
my wings to fly.

How silly

How silly of me to think I would have died.
It sure felt like pain was pinning me to the floor,
but man, being a human makes me incredibly strong.
And I sure do love living.

Soulmate Collector

I am the soulmate collector.
Once you fall into my grasp,
I will never let you go.
But how is it so
that you have left me alone?
I held on so tight.
My soul will never loosen the grip on you,
yet you might have slipped away.

But you will be in my soul
until I fall
old and gray.
And I still hope
you will see me that way
one day.
And perhaps come back
as we decay.

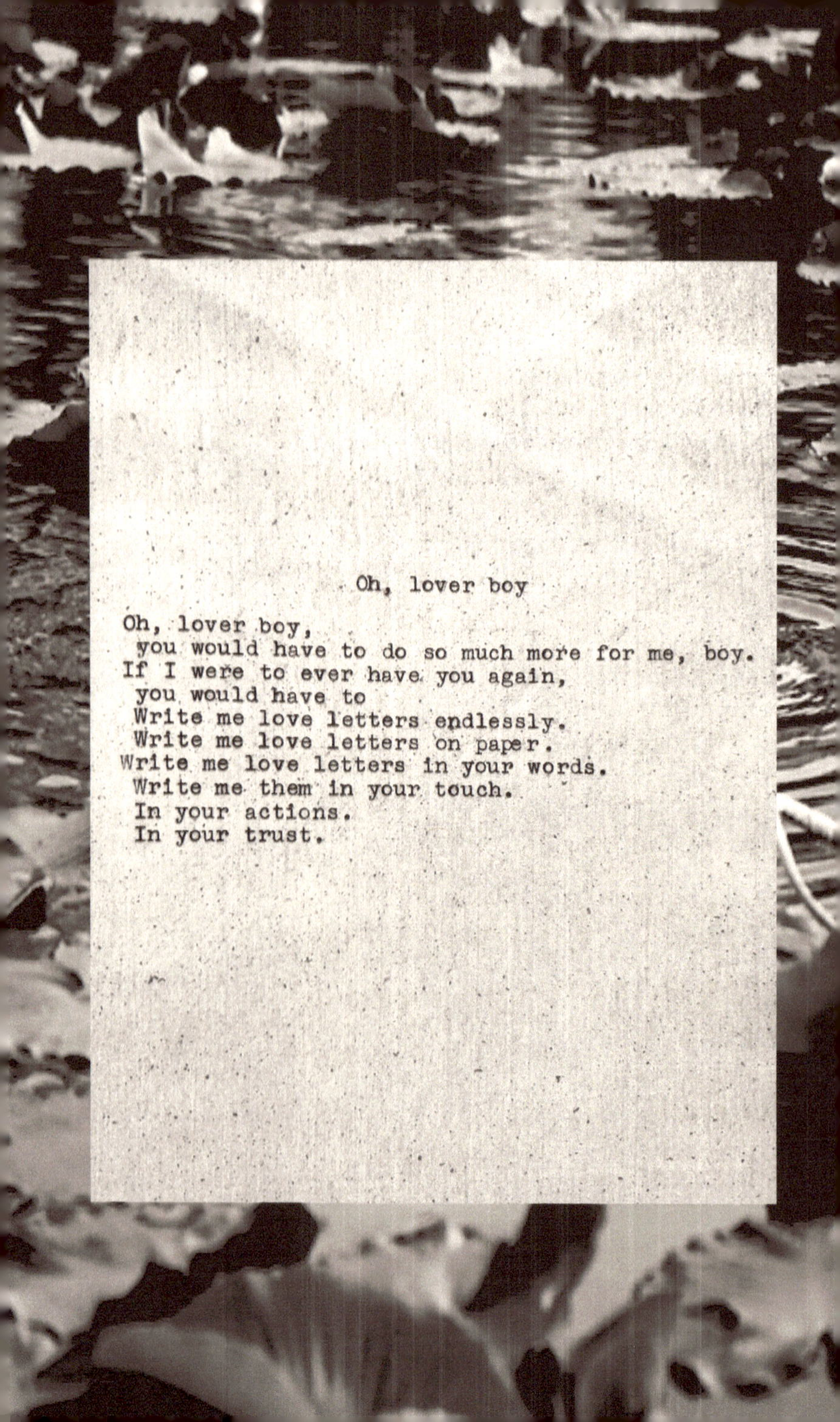
Oh, lover boy

Oh, lover boy,
 you would have to do so much more for me, boy.
If I were to ever have you again,
 you would have to
 Write me love letters endlessly.
 Write me love letters on paper.
Write me love letters in your words.
 Write me them in your touch.
 In your actions.
 In your trust.

Lasso the moon

I'm finding it is okay to let go a little more
because it is nearly impossible
to reach for the moon,

for the moon still shines for you,
but it has its dim days, too
and it cannot be lassoed
when it does not want to.

Sometimes it is full and the rope slips right off;
sometimes it wanes and I can hook a bit of it,
but it is forever going through its phases
and cannot always be in my reach.

Icarus

They said not to fly too close to the sun
but Icarus cannot be the only one.
Love the ones who feel like sunshine
and risk your skin growing blushed
from sincerity.
Live endless days to love your heart out
as if the sun will never return.
Mustn't it be better to love hard
and be burned among the surface
than to fear the rays
for the rest of your days?
My body will feel lighter from the lack of your touch.
The sun may set
but never in a rush.

Naked

Her body is not the only thing
that can be naked.
She is vulnerable to you,
insides spilling out,
and she never regrets a thing.
She is art
and her soul is truly bare to you.
You know her beyond her body,
so do not spare a memory
of her naked complexion.

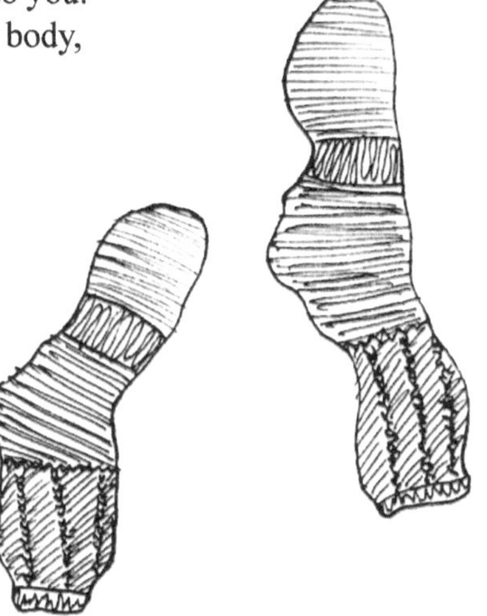

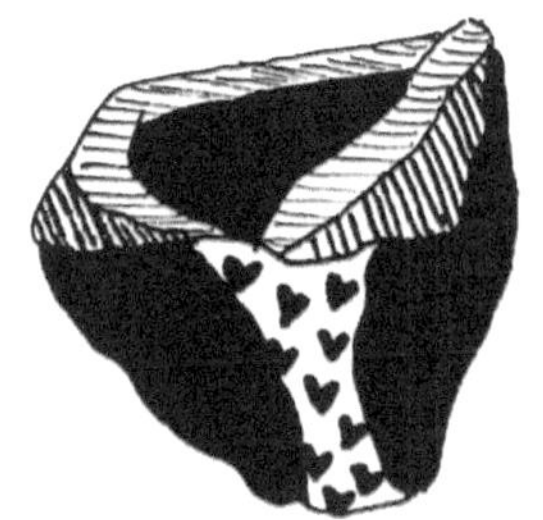

The girl

When I think of this girl
I imagine she feels like a drop of sunshine
She laughs with the pure air of the earth
The way she cares is probably gentle
Even when she feels as blue as the ocean
Romance whirls in the thought of her
I feel like a child with this crush
A simple fool in love or forevermore a desire

Metamorphosis

We are meant to change, my dear.

From lovely little caterpillars,
into beaming things with wings,
we have found our way out,
no longer the same.
Yet we are still equally as beautiful,
just simply meant for the change,
no longer the same lovely things,
for now we have wings
and we must follow our own dreams.

A moth and a butterfly are similar indeed,
yet this time,
in this life cycle,
we were meant to share the same leaf.
Now the skies take us elsewhere.

Give me a flower boy

Give me a flower boy.
A boy with flowers in his hair
and freckles that make up the shape of a daisy.
A boy that smells like daffodils and lilacs
and is as gentle as a lily.
A boy who is rooted in kindness
and grows with each season.
Give me a flower boy.

The wind blows

The wind blows
and my trouble slows
as I type new notes.
A leaf in my typewriter.
Did you leave it there?
Even if you did not,
I like to imagine you did.
The keys smell like your basement
and that old clangy cash register.
I write my heart out,
vintage in my soul,
and your memory floats along.

Today, I am happy

Today, I am happy
as the sun shines and I sit outside
in a flowy and colorful skirt.
A day with bugs
and birds that chirp,
ice cream and food—
soul food for my brain too.
Today, I am happy
and I enjoy that indeed.
Today, I am happy
and I feel like a seed,
sprouting anew—finally—
through the dew.
Today, I am happy,
wiggling my body to tunes,
or simply the air, as I people-watch
because, today, I am happy
and I smile to myself,
glitter on my body
as I feel warm outside and in.
Today, I am happy
and that makes me grin.
I hear chiming in the distance,
magical it seems.
I don't know from where,
but regardless, I gleam
for today,
I am happy.

If you would like to further support Kendall, please take a moment to leave reviews on Goodreads, Barnes & Noble, and Amazon. Thank you.

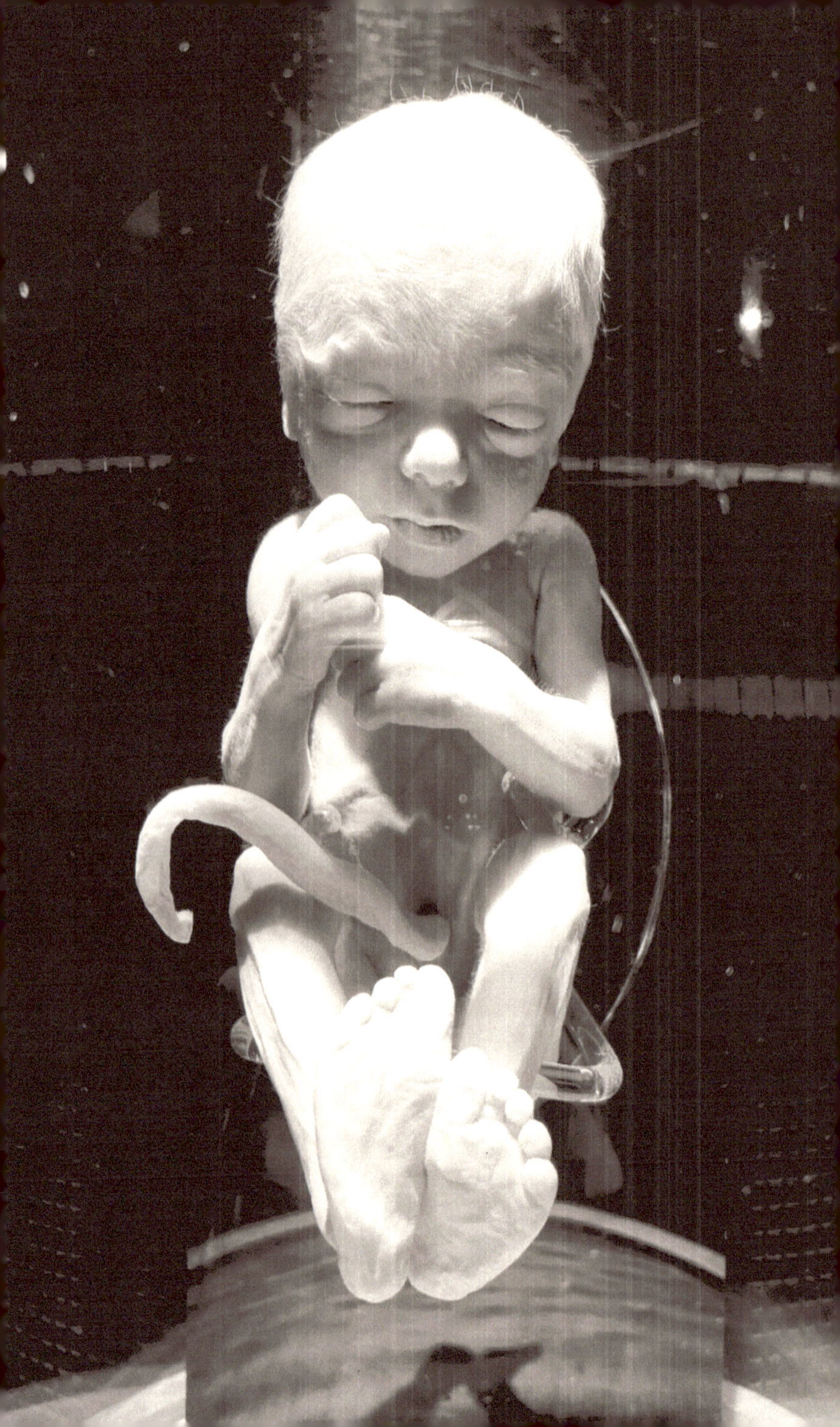

**"Isn't it odd. We can only see our outsides,
but nearly everything happens on the inside"**

- Charlie Mackesy,
The Boy, the Mole, the Fox and the Horse

May this playlist connect you to my soul, as well as your own.

The Willow Weepings

JOURNAL
OF THE
ANTHROPOLOGICAL
INSTITUTE
VOL. XVIII.
1888.-89.
JOURNAL
OF THE
ANTHROPOLOGICAL
INSTITUTE.
VOL. XIX.
1889.-90.
GN
2
R88
v.18
GN
2
R88
v.19

Notes

"Alice in her bottle" is inspired by *Alice in Wonderland.*

"Blue Hornworm" is inspired by both *Alice in Wonderland* and
Alice's Adventures in Wonderland.

"Fish in a cage" inspired by the song *Rule #4* by Fish in a Birdcage.

"Pocket posies" inspired by the children's rhyme
Ring around the Rosie.

"The old moth that lives in a shoe" inspired by the children's rhyme
There was an Old Woman Who Lived in a Shoe.

Acknowledgments

I have the deepest of thanks, once again, to Flor Ana. Flor is my mentor, creator of Indie Earth Publishing, and most importantly, a close friend of mine. You inspire so much creativity in my days and my continuous growth as an author. I deeply appreciate your efforts and help with my published works, more than I can ever explain. Thank you for everything you do for me and the Indie Earth family I am so lucky to be part of.

Thank you to my fellow Indie Earth authors and the creative community I have found myself a part of in person and online. Locally and distant, you are all so amazing, kind, and talented. Thank you for supporting and seeing my deep connection to life and my art.

Thank you to anyone who has witnessed or enjoyed my poetry and art. No matter the connection, I appreciate the interest in what I share to the world. Thank you for seeing the beauty in myself and my words. I am immensely grateful for every opportunity and experience being an author has brought me and I do not take it for granted. I am so lucky to be chasing my dreams and having such beauty be a reality in my life.

Thank you to life, love, growth, and vulnerability.

My heartfelt recognition to you all.

About The Author

Kendall Hope is a Colorado native, who thrives off of sunshine and has been a creative since the time she was small. She loves exploring the outdoors and being a part of nature, which translates into her poetry. In 2022, she debuted as an author with her poetry collection *Pockets of Lavender* and has gone on to be featured in a variety of anthologies including *Unsent Love Letters: An Anthology of Words Left Unspoken, The Spell Jar: Poetry for the Modern Witch*, and *Glow: Self-Care Poetry for the Soul*. Kendall's works have also been featured in local stores in Colorado Springs, like Poor Richard's, Ivywild School, and Eclectic CO.

Visit www.kendallhopepoetry.com to learn more.

Or visit Kendall on Instagram at @kendallhopepoetry

Author Photo: Katie Scruggs-Galloway ©

About The Publisher

Indie Earth Publishing is an author-first, independent publishing company based in Miami, FL, dedicated to giving artists and writers the creative freedom they deserve in publishing their poetry, fiction, and short stories. We provide our authors a plethora of services that are meant to make them feel like they are finally releasing the book of their dreams, including professional editing, design, formatting, organization, advanced reader teams, and so much more. With Indie Earth Publishing, you're more than just another author, you're part of the Indie Earth creative family, making a difference in the world, one book at a time.

www.indieearthbooks.com

For inquiries, please email:
indieearthpublishinghouse@gmail.com

Instagram: @indieearthbooks

* 9 7 9 8 9 8 8 0 3 7 9 4 1 *